FORMS OF GOVERNMENT: NEED TO KNOW

DEMOCRACY

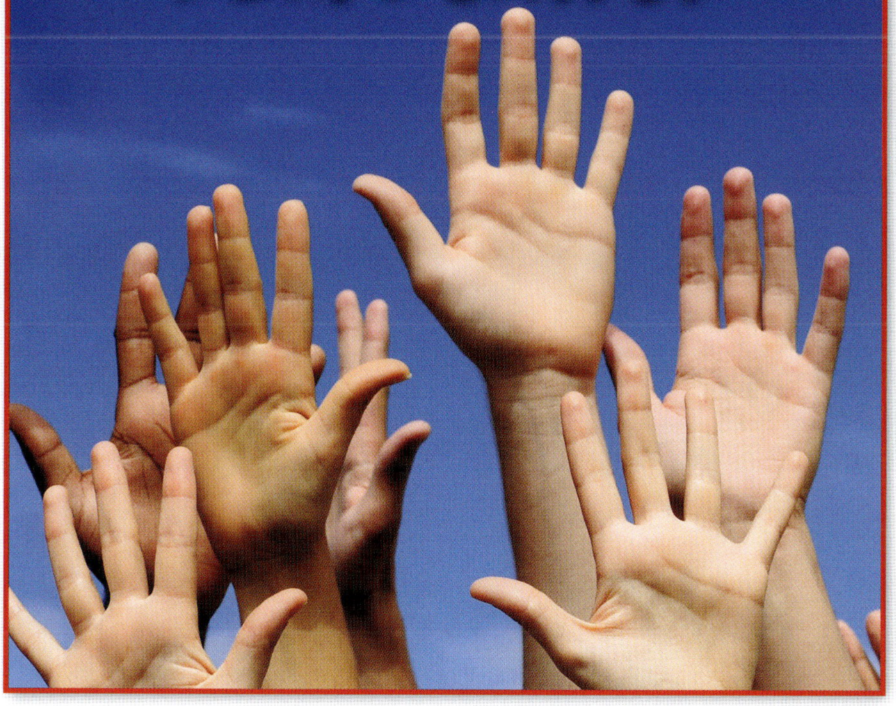

by D. R. Faust

Consultant: Caitlin Krieck, Social Studies Teacher and Instructional Coach, The Lab School of Washington

SilverTip Books, an imprint of Bearport Publishing by FlutterBee

Credits
Cover and title page, © mangostock/iStock; 3, © PeskyMonkey/Shutterstock; 4–5, © Prostock-Studio/iStock; 7T, © AnnaStills/iStock; 7B, © Mircea Moira/Shutterstock; 9, © Alan Mazzocco/Shutterstock; 11, © Monkey Business Images/Shutterstock; 13, © Rob Crandall/Shutterstock; 15, © TERESA SUAREZ/Getty Images; 17, © Zoomtraveller/Shutterstock; 19, © Kyodo/Associated Press; 21, © De Luan/Alamy Stock Photo; 22–23, © Artepics/Alamy Stock Photo; 25, © IanDagnall Computing/Alamy Stock Photo; 27, © Daniel Hoz/Shutterstock.

Bearport Publishing Company Product Development Team
Kayla Eggert, Theresa Emminizer, Kim Jones, Allison Juda, Cole Nelson, Naomi Reich, Steve Scheluchin, Tiana Tran

Statement on Usage of Generative Artificial Intelligence
Bearport Publishing remains committed to publishing high-quality nonfiction books. Therefore, we restrict the use of generative AI to ensure accuracy of all text and visual components pertaining to a book's subject. See BearportPublishing.com for details.

Library of Congress Cataloging-in-Publication Data is available at www.loc.gov or upon request from the publisher.

ISBN: 979-8-89577-635-3 (hardcover)
ISBN: 979-8-89577-789-3 (paperback)
ISBN: 979-8-89577-723-7 (ebook)

For more information, write to Bearport Publishing, 3500 American Blvd W, Suite 150, Bloomington, MN 55431. Printed in the United States of America.

Contents

Who Decides?

You and your friends want to watch a movie. How do you pick which one? Does everyone get to be part of the choice? If so, that's a democracy. In this form of government, the people get a say in decisions.

Everyone having a say doesn't mean everyone agrees. It also doesn't mean everybody gets their way. Maybe more people want to watch a horror flick than a comedy. Then, horror wins.

By the People

The word *democracy* means rule by the people. In this form of government, the people have a voice in how things will go.

This can happen at any level of government. A democracy can be used for a small school board. It can also be the system for an entire country.

There are many forms of government. The main difference between them is who has the power. Most governments are actually a mix of systems. They use aspects from different kinds of government structures.

There are different ways people may give their opinions in democracies. Sometimes, ideas are spoken about publicly. Other times, they are written down and kept **anonymous**.

Most democracies use some form of voting. The right to vote is called **suffrage**.

Historically, democracies have not always given everyone the right to vote. In the United States, only white men were allowed to vote until 1870. Over time, Black men got suffrage. Finally, women received voting rights.

Voting is a way to participate in a democracy.

Who's In Charge Here?

There are two basic kinds of democracy. They have people make different kinds of decisions.

In a direct democracy, the people make all the choices themselves. For example, they may vote on the laws everyone has to follow.

Direct democracies are most commonly found with smaller groups. That is because giving everyone a direct say can take time. It is easier with fewer people.

In a **representative** democracy, the people choose representatives. These are the **officials** who run the government. Representatives make decisions about laws. They are supposed to represent, or stand in for, the people. These lawmakers are responsible for having their communities' best interests in mind.

In the U.S. government, there are two groups of lawmakers. The Senate has two representatives from each state. The number of lawmakers in the House of Representatives is different. It is based on the population of each state.

Sometimes, United States lawmakers all come together in a joint session.

Leading the People

Within a representative democracy, the person in charge of the government is called the head of government. There can also be a head of state. This is the person who speaks for the country when talking with other global leaders. Sometimes, these jobs are held by the same person.

The head of government often has a lot of power. However, the head of state can be a **ceremonial** role. This leader is more of a symbol. They may have little say in governing.

G7 summits allow some world leaders to come together to talk about global issues.

At the Head

Who decides on the heads of government or state? It depends on the type of democracy. A **republic** is a representative democracy. In this system, the people vote for the head of government.

In a parliamentary (*paar*-luh-MEN-tr-ee) democracy, people choose representative lawmakers. They form a **parliament**. Then, this group picks their leader.

The leader in a republic is usually called a president. A parliamentary democracy has a head of government called a prime minister.

Canada's parliament building in Ottawa

In a **constitutional monarchy**, there is a royal head of state. They are not elected. But there are also representatives that have been voted into **office**. The elected officials have the power to make laws. The royal head of state acts as a face for the country.

Japan has a constitutional monarchy. The emperor of Japan is the head of state. But political power is held by the people in a parliament.

Naruhito *(left)* is the emperor of Japan. Shigeru Ishiba *(right)* is the prime minister.

Long History

People have formed democracies since before the time of written records. These early democracies could be found in Asia, India, and Northern Africa.

Ancient Greece is often considered the birthplace of modern democracy. This kind of government developed around 500 BCE. The voters used a direct democracy.

One of the oldest democracies still around is the Haudenosaunee (hoh-DEE-noh-shoh-nee) Confederacy. This group in North America is made up of six Native American nations.

All free male citizens could vote in Athens in ancient Greece.

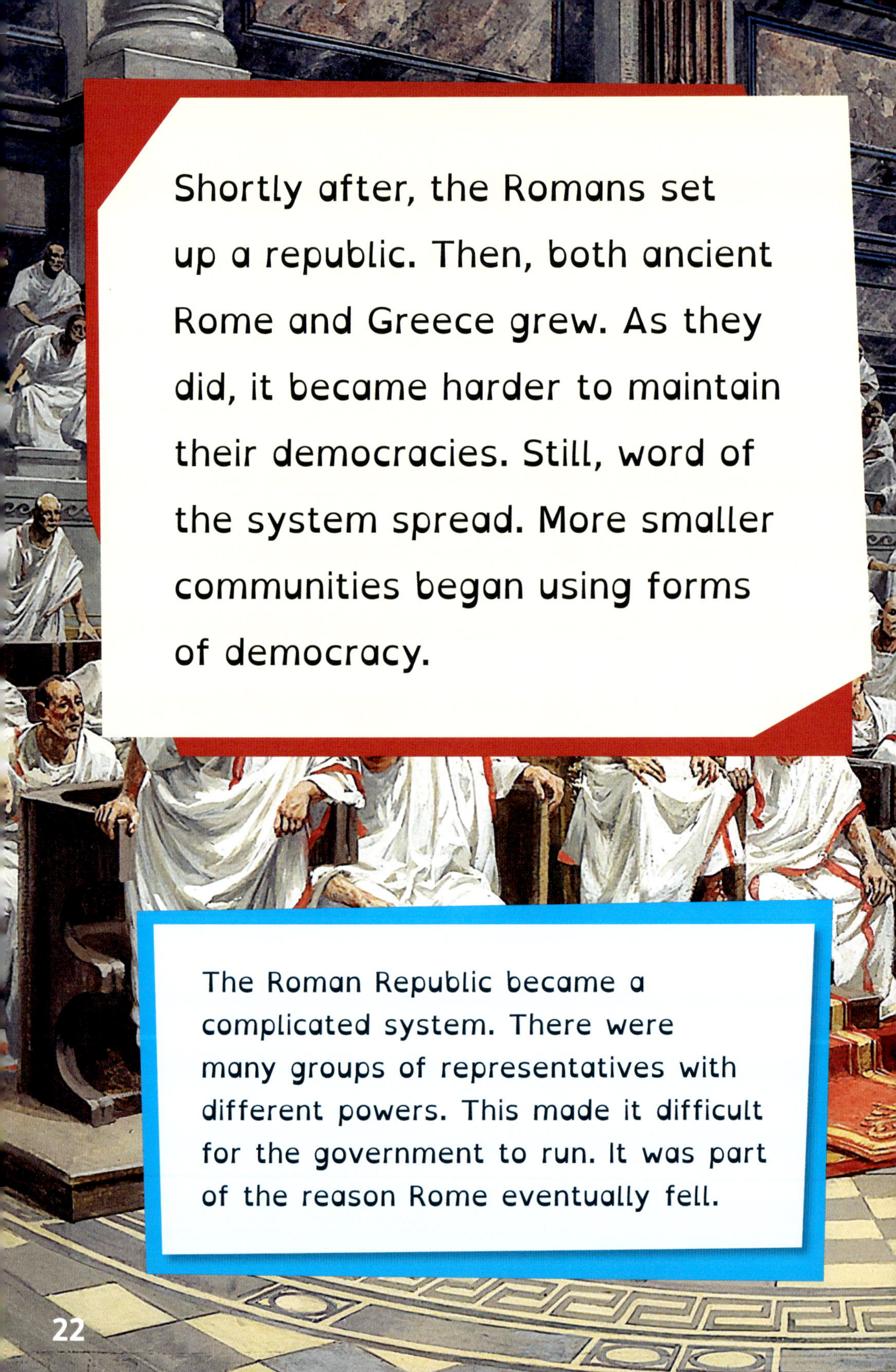

Shortly after, the Romans set up a republic. Then, both ancient Rome and Greece grew. As they did, it became harder to maintain their democracies. Still, word of the system spread. More smaller communities began using forms of democracy.

The Roman Republic became a complicated system. There were many groups of representatives with different powers. This made it difficult for the government to run. It was part of the reason Rome eventually fell.

The Roman Senate

Democracy Spreads

During the 1700s, democracy was on the rise. People wanted more of a say in their government.

As democracy spread, it changed. More places tried representative democracies. Over time, more people got the right to vote. New laws also allowed more people to hold office.

In 1776, the 13 **colonies** in North America separated from Great Britain. They formed the United States. The new country became a democratic republic. This inspired similar movements in France and Haiti.

The founders of the United States

Democracy Today

Advances in technology have continued to change democracy. They let people communicate faster. Ideas can travel the world with the tap of a button. What people want and need from their governments today can change quickly. And democracy will likely change as this happens.

Social media can be a powerful tool in a democracy. It is used to quickly spread news and information. Social media also helps voters organize. People can easily come together for a cause.

Forms of Democracy

Democracy comes in many forms. Each puts power in the hands of the people. But the way these governments run is slightly different.

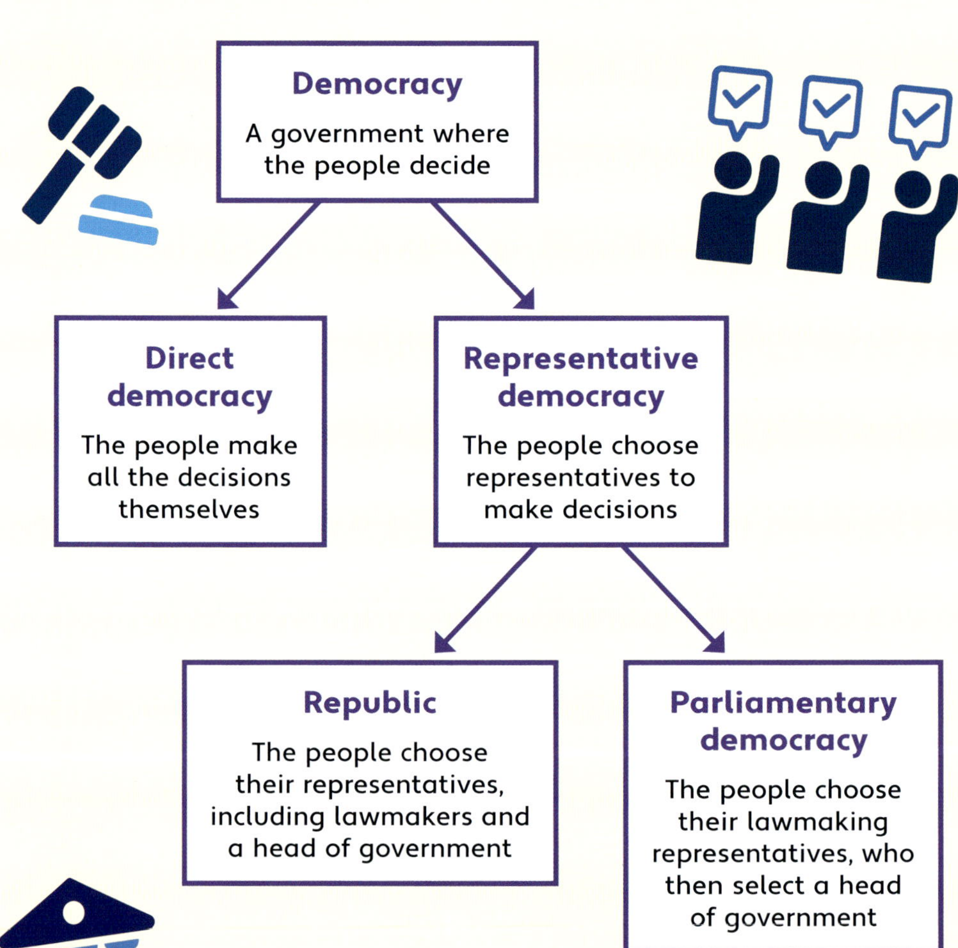

SilverTips for SUCCESS

★SilverTips for REVIEW

Review what you've learned. Use the text to help you.

Define key terms

constitutional monarchy
direct democracy
parliamentary democracy
representative democracy
republic

Check for understanding

What is the key difference between a direct democracy and a representative democracy?

Explain the roles of the head of state and head of government.

Name two systems of representational democracy.

Think deeper

How might your life be different if the style of government in your city, state, or nation changed?

★SilverTips for TAKING TESTS

- **Make a study plan.** Ask your teacher what the test is going to cover. Then, set aside time to study a little bit every day.
- **Read all the questions carefully.** Be sure you know what is being asked.
- **Skip any questions** you don't know how to answer right away. Mark them and come back later if you have time.

Glossary

anonymous not named or identified

ceremonial visually symbolic but without real power or influence

colonies areas that have been settled by people from another country and are ruled by that original country

constitutional monarchy a form of government in which a country is ruled by a king or a queen whose power is limited by a constitution

office a position held by members of the government

officials people who hold an office or important position

parliament a group of people who have been elected to make laws

representative standing in for or speaking for a larger group

republic a government where individuals are elected to represent groups of people

suffrage the right to vote

Read More

Faust, Daniel R. *The Senate (U.S. Government: Need to Know)*. Minneapolis: Bearport Publishing, 2022.

Gunderson, Jessica. *History Tipsters Go to the Polls: The Inside Scoop on Voting and Elections (History Tipsters)*. North Mankato, MN: Capstone Press, 2024.

Sjonger, Rebecca. *Democracy and Other Forms of Government (Choosing Democracy)*. New York: Crabtree Publishing, 2023.

Learn More Online

1. Go to **FactSurfer.com** or scan the QR code below.
2. Enter "**Democracy**" into the search box.
3. Click on the cover of this book to see a list of websites.

Index

About the Author

D. R. Faust is a freelance writer of fiction and nonfiction. They live in Queens, NY.